Joseph Warren Alden

Emancipation and Emigration

a plan to transfer the freedmen of the South to the government lands of

the West

Joseph Warren Alden

Emancipation and Emigration
a plan to transfer the freedmen of the South to the government lands of the West

ISBN/EAN: 9783337284978

Printed in Europe, USA, Canada, Australia, Japan

Cover: Foto ©Andreas Hilbeck / pixelio.de

More available books at **www.hansebooks.com**

Principia Club Papers, No. 9.

EMANCIPATION AND EMIGRATION.

A

PLAN TO TRANSFER

THE

FREEDMEN OF THE SOUTH

TO THE

GOVERNMENT LANDS OF THE WEST.

BOSTON, MASS.:
PUBLISHED BY THE PRINCIPIA CLUB.
1878.

CONTENTS.

SPECIAL NOTICE.

The PRINCIPIA CLUB PAPERS consist of nine chapters, to wit:

Vaticanism Unmasked, ...	Chaps. 1 and 2
The Political Trinity of Despotism, ...	Chap. 3
Despotism vs. Republicanism, ...	Chap. 4
The Ballot a Sacred Trust, ...	Chap. 5
The Political Trinity Victorious, ...	Chap. 6
The Southern Policy a Failure, ...	Chap. 7
Finance, Politics, and Religion, ...	Chap. 8
Emancipation and Emigration : a Plan to Colonize and Settle the Freedmen of the South on the Government Lands of the West, ...	Chap. 9

All these chapters, or papers, make a book of 344 pages, and will be sold for $1.00.

N. B. — Orders should be addressed " J. W. ALDEN, President of the Principia Club, No. 9 Hanson Street, Boston, Mass."

AN OPEN LETTER TO THE FREEDMEN OF THE SOUTH.

CAMBRIDGEPORT, MASS., Aug. 13, 1878.

Fellow Citizens:—If any apology for improving your condition were needed it may be found in the fact that a large portion of the last forty years of my life was spent, and many thousand dollars invested, in the terrible conflict with the slave power. It is *not* necessary for me to remind you that the result of that conflict was your emancipation from American slavery by the Republican party, with such leaders and co-laborers as Chief Justice Salmon P. Chase, Senators Charles Sumner and Henry Wilson, Rev. Joshua Leavitt, D. D., and Rev. Wm. Goodell, all of whom have now passed away, but whose life-long labors, with many who are still living, culminated in the Emancipation Proclamation of President Lincoln in 1863. But it *is*, as it seems to me, necessary to remind you that the Republican party of to-day is a very different thing from then—that your liberties and citizenship have now become the stock in trade of corrupt politicians—that your political rights have been bartered away for the *promises* of your old masters, which they never meant to perform when they made them, and for which they now substitute *demands* for your return to slavery, with the pecuniary interest of one to two thousand dollars in each able-bodied man *left out;* consequently when they shoot a man they do not lose that amount of investment in his body. Among the demands of the "dominant race" is the repeal of the constitutional amendments which made you citizens and gave you the ballot. Of course they did not ask the Republican party to do it *directly.* They only asked them to put the political power of the nation into the hands of the Democratic party, and the second and third rate politicians now at the head of affairs at Washington were stupid enough to do it, for the poor privilege of occupying the White House for a short time. But when another Congress assembles with a Democratic majority

4

in both houses (if such a calamity should overtake us), that will be done as sure as water runs down hill. Now what we propose to do is to open a door to the "better land" of this country, into which every freedman, who has had enough of slavery, both *legal* before the war, and *practical* since, and who has enterprise enough to desire to better his condition and that of his family, if he has one, may enter. It is the most practical, sensible, and scientific " labor reform" yet proposed ; with neither the blatherskite of Kearney, nor his blasphemy, profanity, nor blarney, to mar and jeopardize the movement.

It has been known in Washington for some time, that " The Principia Club Papers, No. 9," soon to be issued, will contain a plan of emigration for the freedmen and their families of the Southern States, and their settlement upon the government lands of the Northern and Western States and Territories, where they can cultivate their own farms and sit under their own vine and fig-tree. The club will appoint a board of trustees in whom the public can have the utmost confidence, whose duty it shall be to assist the freedmen in the selection, purchase, and payment of their farms, and the removal of their families and outfits.

More full explanations and descriptions will be given in the pamphlet, which will contain also specific directions to individuals or colonies how to proceed in the matter. While arrangements are being made with the government, the club will be glad to receive any suggestions from any one interested in the movement, and especially the leading colored men in the country.

Concerning this movement, any information desired may be had by addressing the president of the club,

J. W. ALDEN,
No. 9 Hanson Street, Boston, Mass.

EMANCIPATION AND EMIGRATION.

When emancipation took place, in 1863, it was not thought, by the noble army of philanthropists who had labored more than a quarter of a century for its accomplishment, that it would ever be necessary for the freedmen to flee their native States, in order to enjoy their civil and political rights and privileges under the Constitution.

Nor was it ever dreamed by the voting Republicans of 1876, that the administration they were putting into power could ever become so stupid as to surrender the national power into the hands of the rebel States, under so thin a guise as the old exploded humbug of South Carolina nullification — State rights, home-rule doctrine ; and then stand by with folded arms and see the freedmen deliberately turned over to the tender mercies of the political trinity of despotism, to be stripped of their civil and political rights under the Constitution, and to be refused protection by the national government. It made no difference that the robbers were *rebels* and the robbed *loyal* citizens. The hollow promises of the rebels who had fought four years to destroy the government, it seems, were better currency at Washington than the protests of the loyal people who had saved it.

But the fifteen years that have elapsed since emancipation, have demonstrated the fact that these loyal people' who fought for and saved the government, and who voted for and elected the present administration, must be returned to practical slavery, submit to serfdom, or emigrate to more civilized States, where their civil and political rights will be cheerfully accorded to them.

The proof of this proposition lies in the fact that State after State, in the South, which had amended their antebellum constitutions, so as to conform to that of the United States, preparatory to their readmission to the Union after the war, have, since their admission, remodelled the said constitutions in the interest of the " dominant class of white rulers." Moreover, the leaders of that

1*

same class are now in hot haste to have the United States
Constitution made to conform to their own State laws,
by the repeal of the amendments enfranchising the freedmen,—a specimen of sharp practice and unparalleled
audacity, only equalled in the papal church, where the
hierarchy made their system, and then a translation of
the Bible to fit into it, instead of making a system to
conform to the Bible, as originally written. (See Vati-
canism Unmasked.)

If " the dominant race," as Mr. Gordon called them at
the Revere House dinner, with the approval of Governor
Rice and company, choose to put their carts before their
donkeys, in their own States, they can do so, but when
they call upon the nation to do it, the North may have a
word to say about it.

If that "dominant race" we have heard so much about,
and of which we have had such sad specimens in the
present Congress, are expecting to get their potatoes
dug, their corn hoed, and their cotton picked, for a peck
of corn or so per week to each laborer, as their fathers
have done for a couple of centuries past, we beg leave to
differ from them, and suggest to their laborers a more
excellent way for themselves. More than this : we propose to assist those who desire a better condition, to
obtain it quietly, where each can enjoy the fruits of his
own labors, and sit with his family under his own vine
and fig-tree, man fashion, and where their wives and
daughters will not be stripped and receive upon their
bare backs, for some petty offence, as many lashes as the
" dominant race" may please to inflict, as was the practice under the old slave code, and is still continued.

The whipping-post is as yet an institution of the slave
oligarchy, if we may credit the following telegram :—

"At Hampton, Virginia, the other day, a white girl
of fourteen years received fifteen lashes at the whipping-
post for stealing a pair of shoes."

If the "white girl of fourteen years" had stolen, instead of a pair of shoes, the assets of a bank, railroad,
or any other corporation, she would have been wined and

dined according to the present moral code of the solid South, which is being copied all over the country. If our Northern readers feel that we have overdrawn the picture, and " flaunted the bloody shirt," we beg them to remember that the Southern press furnishes the material for that article. The last Boston paper we happened to take up while writing, has the following quotation from the " Oskoloua (Mississippi) Southern States ":—

"The future belongs to us and ours. Davis and his Cabinet and his soldiers will rank with the Washingtons, the Hampdens, and the Tells in the Pantheon of history, while Grant and his horde of bloody hirelings will be classed with the Vandals, Goths, and Huns." ·

We will refer the reader to the " Appendix " of this, No. 9, for further evidence of the public sentiment at the South, which goes to show that the freedmen must EMIGRATE, FIGHT, or PERISH.

While the churches of the North are sending missionaries to educate them up to the point of Christian citizenship and an educated ballot, the " dominant white race " are robbing them of their political rights, shooting them down, if they dare to assert them, and making them "hewers of wood and drawers of water," as in the olden times of American slavery. (See Appendix for evidence of this.)

PREAMBLE AND RESOLUTIONS.

The following preamble and resolutions, with plan of operations, will indicate the work we propose to be done, or at least entered upon.

PREAMBLE.

Whereas, by the proclamation of emancipation of President Lincoln in the year 1863, about four million of colored people were emancipated from American slavery ; and *whereas*, by the subsequent amendments to the Constitution of the United States, passed by Congress and ratified by more than three-quarters of the States of the Union, nearly a million of said emancipated slaves, of lawful age and sex, were enfranchised and made citizens ; and

Whereas, said amendments to the Constitution were practically nullified and rendered a dead letter in the Southern States at the last presidential election, and ever since, by disfranchising the colored Republicans who would not put into the ballot-boxes Democratic tickets, shooting some and intimidating others ; and

Whereas, the elements of despotism in the Democratic party are now clamoring for a repeal of the said constitutional amendments, so that they may return the colored Republicans legally to their former condition, or a worse one, and use them for Democratic voters and ballot-box stuffers ; therefore, —

RESOLUTIONS.

1. *Resolved*, That the Principia Club appeal to the government of the country, to render such assistance as will enable their emancipated people to take their families to the Northern and Western States and Territories, and settle on government lands, where they can enjoy their rights of citizenship, and be protected by the government which has thus far failed to render them protection from bull-dozing, assassination, intimidation, and other barbarisms to which they are now subjected by the elements of despotism in the South.

2. *Resolved*, That a board of trustees be appointed to assist the freedmen in obtaining their lands at government price, together with such an outfit as will enable them to remove their families and commence farming on their own account, to receive and disburse all moneys contributed for the above purposes, appoint such agents as may be necessary in the several States, to promote emigration and carry forward the following plan of operations, until the freedmen and their families who desire it, shall be removed to better homes and more civilized society, entirely away from the barbarism of slavery, and the pernicious doctrine that States rights are supreme and national rights are subordinate.

3. *Resolved*, That emancipation from American slav-

ery being practically nullified, therefore, emancipation from home rule as understood and practised at the South, becomes a *necessity*, and emigration to a civilized community a consequence.

4. *Resolved*, That the President of the Principia Club be instructed to obtain from the Secretary of the Interior a list of the number of acres of unsold and unpre-empted lands in each of the Northern and Western States and Territories, from which the Trustees may select farms for their wards.

5. *Resolved*, That the same ascertain from the officers of the Pacific and other railroads, the best terms they are prepared to offer to settlers for the transportation of themselves, their families, and their outfits to the lands along their roads respectively.

6. *Resolved*, That the twenty-eight million acres of land contiguous to the Central, Union, Kansas and Denver Pacific roads, which the Secretary of the Interior has recently decided to open to actual settlers, at the government price of $1.25 per acre (the three years' limitation after the completion of said roads contained in the landgrant laws having expired), shall receive the special attention of the Trustees of this association in the selection of farms for applicants. But in case the decision of the Secretary of the Interior should not stand, or should be contested, then the government lands will be purchased instead.

7. *Resolved*, That the Republican party, to whom the country owes, under God, Emancipation, be called upon to finish the work so nobly begun, by carrying out a provision of the United States Constitution, Art. IV., Sect. II., Clause I., which reads, "the citizens of each State shall be entitled to all privileges and immunities of citizens in the several States," and that this clause of the Constitution, together with the amendments enfranchising the freedmen, be made test questions at the polls, until a solid North shall elect a government that will have backbone enough to see to it that every State in the Union shall strictly comply with the requirements of

the United States Constitution, or revert to a territorial condition.

THE PLAN OF OPERATIONS.

1. The Trustees shall be men of either known wealth, ability, financial strength, or business capacity, in whose honesty and integrity the community will have the most implicit confidence.

2. All moneys entrusted to them shall be appropriated in strict conformity to the directions of the donor or lender, whether for the general expenses or the purchase of lands.

3. The funds furnished the Trustees for the purchase of lands, shall be treated as loans or donations as the party may elect, the deed in each case to be taken in the name of the party furnishing the money to pay for the land, which deed may be held by the Trustees, or passed over to the owner as he may elect, as security, if for a loan.

The terms of sale to the freedmen by the Trustees shall be substantially those of the pre-emption laws, to wit: $1.25 per acre; but the terms of payment may be mutually arranged between the owner and purchaser, or their agents, the Trustees.

5. Every freedman who can pay for his own farm may have his deed at once, and enjoy the privileges granted to and by this association, by the payment of five dollars towards the general expenses.

By the above plan it will be seen that any person investing fifty dollars for a quarter section, one hundred dollars for a half section, or two hundred dollars for a section, and so on, will hold the land as security at $1.25 per acre, while the alternate sections which have been sold by the Pacific railroads have averaged much more, or about five dollars an acre (some have sold for fifteen dollars). Thus it will be seen that the investment will be a safe one, and at the same time facilitate the exodus of the freedmen to the Western States.

The Trustees will not be allowed to run the association in debt, but will invest the money put into their hands in the best lands, according to their judgment, and sell them to the freedmen in the order in which application and selection is made.

Justice to the freedmen, after the treatment they have received, requires that the United States government should transport them free of charge, together with their families, household goods, farming implements, &c., to unpre-empted lands in the Western States and Territories, giving to each family land sufficient for their maintenance, with due diligence and care, and a reasonable time to pay for it. But the prospect of a "labor reform" movement of that magnitude does not look very encouraging, when we remember that the rebel South have thirty-five bogus members in Congress, to which they are not entitled, while depriving large Republican majorities of several States of the exercise of the elective franchise, which the amendments to the Constitution conferred upon them.

If we had more STATESMEN in Congress, and fewer corrupt politicians, the prospect would be more flattering that the demands of justice would be heeded.

If, however, the government as at present constituted, should take hold of the matter in earnest and good faith, our "National Farmers' Association" may be easily modified to conform to the circumstances. But on the other hand, if the "solid South," by virtue of its *thirty-five* bogus representatives, should rule the nation as in ante-bellum times it did with its *twenty-five*, neither the freedmen nor their friends can expect any thing to be done in the direction we have suggested that will benefit the freedmen, until Congress shall be reconstructed at the polls, or until the large Republican majorities of freedmen in the South, despairing of the protection of their political rights by the Federal power, seize their last resort and defend them by their own strong arms, under "home rule and State rights." If they should do this the "dominant race" and their rifle clubs would vanish like dew before the sun, and that ball wouldn't stop rolling until the whole nest of Southern rebels are cleaned out.

But we propose to the government to prevent all this bloodshed, and quietly remove the freedmen and their families to the Western prairies.

SAFETY AS AN INVESTMENT.

1. When an individual furnishes the Trustees with money to purchase a farm of a quarter section or more, for a freedman and his family, he will get, in due time, a deed of the land at $1.25 per acre, as security for his investment. The investor may then sell the land to the farmer or freedman on such terms of payment as may be agreed upon; or, if more convenient, the Trustees will do it, under his instructions.

2. When a purchaser of a farm pays for it himself he will get his deed at once, and that will end the matter with him, so far as the Trustees are concerned.

3. Parties wishing to *donate* farms for poor and worthy freedmen and their families, can do so through the Trustees, and be furnished in due time with the names of the recipients, their location, and post-office address.

4. As an investment, well-located farms at $1.25 per acre, are as safe as government bonds, and will pay a much larger interest. We have already stated that the lands donated to the Pacific railroads have *averaged* five dollars per acre, while some of them have sold as high as fifteen dollars per acre.

OBJECTIONS CONSIDERED.

1. We are aware that one objection to our plan of placing the freedmen in a comparatively independent position from their old masters and their posterity, is its

magnitude. But that is no valid reason why it should not be adopted. If it cannot be wholly accomplished in a generation or a century, let it be done, so far as it can be, in our generation, and continued by our successors until it shall be finished.

Under God, Moses undertook to lead the children of Israel out of Egyptian bondage into the promised land. In doing it they were forty years in the wilderness, but in due time the thing was accomplished and passed into history. The magnitude of the project and the time required for its accomplishment were no objections to its being undertaken. It is true we have no Moses to lead the freedmen into our western prairies, but we have the same God to work under that Moses had.

2. The American Board of Commissioners for Foreign Missions, when it began its work, had no expectation of converting the world to Christianity in a generation or a century; but that was no reason why it should not organize and go to work, leaving for its successors to finish what it then only began. The same is true of the Home Missionary Society work, and that of the American Missionary Association, which has the freedmen under its care especially. The work of both of these societies will be greatly facilitated by taking the freedmen from the clutches of the old slave oligarchy, and placing them in an independent civil position on our boundless prairies, and in cities and villages where they can care for themselves, their families, and their country, with none to molest nor make them afraid; a work which neither of the above societies can do, under their present constitutions.

Where they are, Col. Preston, of Virginia, in a paper addressed to the American Missionary Association at its annual meeting said: "There is no place for them as legislators, and no room for them among the whites as doctors, lawyers, professors, engineers, architects, or artists. By other pursuits they must gain their livelihood, and for other pursuits they must be trained."

It will be observed that agriculture is left out of the colonel's catalogue, and, of course, must be included in the " other pursuits " by which the freedmen " must gain their livelihood." Now we propose to place them on the best farming lands on this continent, where they can not only gain a " livelihood," but qualify themselves for any and all of the above occupations and professions, with no rifle clubs to keep them in subjection to the ruling class of whites.

President Fairchild, of Berea College, said that the above quotation was a " leaden weight hung upon the neck of the colored youth."

Our plan proposes to put them in a position to shake off that " leaden weight," and rise in the scale of humanity in consonance with their just deserts.

It can but commend itself to the friends of the freedmen.

THE PLAN APPROVED.

Since our " open letter to the freedmen of the South," dated Aug. 13, 1878, and published in the Boston " Traveller," a few days after, announcing our plan of emigration, we have received letters of endorsement from leading freedmen, which show the feeling in the South in favor of this plan, and their opposition to the Liberia scheme of emigration. One of them writes us : " I prefer going West, and many hundreds here would join me. I am opposed to emigration to Liberia. We cannot live in the South and enjoy our political rights. We need wealth and education. These are what we cannot get in the South, where the landed aristocrat refuses to sell and divide his land among the blacks. He opposes our education, so as to be able to control our political rights, and make us only " hewers of wood and drawers of water." I hope the plan will be a success. The prayers of many freedmen will go with you and the whole scheme."

This writer is endorsed by Hon. J. H. Rainey, M. C. from South Carolina.

As we go to press with this pamphlet, we will give the key-note of the newspaper press on the subject.

The " Washington Republican " urges upon the colored men of the South that the best thing they can do is to go to the West. It says : —

' " And the sooner they go the better for all concerned. Their exodus from the South would leave the soil of that to them inhospitable section without tillers. It would weaken the political strength of the ex-Confederacy in the Union, and they would stand some chance of being represented in the national councils. as well as being counted in the basis of that representation. Besides, it would awaken a sentiment among the better classes of the South in favor of law and order, for the purpose of persuading them to remain ' at home '; and this would result in a determined effort to overcome Ku-Kluxism and bull-dozing in all their varied forms."

To be " counted in the basis of that representation," and be forced to submit to have bull-dozing representatives sent to Congress by the Ku-Klux, is an unparalleled monstrosity.

THE FREEDMEN'S DANGER.

We verily believe that the chief danger to the freedmen is in being fooled by the *fair promises* of " the dominant white race." They have succeeded so well in befooling the government, and have found out by experience that it is much easier and more profitable to *fool* than to *fight*, that they will try the same game with the freedmen, as soon as they begin to emigrate. *But don't be deceived by them.* You had experience enough, both during slavery and since emancipation, of their perfidy, faithlessness, and treachery. In our forty years' contest with the slave power, we never knew its votaries to make a promise, involving human rights, *and redeem it*, when it was against their pecuniary interest to do so. I may say the same of their political promises, specimens of which are given in the previous numbers of

the Principia Club papers, also in the Appendix, and
need not be repeated in this.

Rebels who claim that this is "a white man's country,"
and that "negroes have no rights that white men are
bound to respect," are not to be trusted. The thirty-five
members of Congress to which the freedmen are entitled,
should be chosen by their votes, and, in every locality
where the freedmen are in a majority, and are fraudu-
lently deprived of their vote, the representative from that
district should be denied a seat in Congress. This would
dispose of the Democratic majority of bull-dozers at once.
But whether this can be done or not, as things now are,
organize into colonies, leave the "solid South to the
world, the flesh, and the devil," emigrate West, where
you can vote and enjoy your political rights, as the
Constitution defines them.

THE NATIONAL FARMERS' ASSOCIATION.

ARTICLE I.

This association shall be called the National Farmers'
Association.

ARTICLE II.

The officers of this association shall consist of a President, Vice-President, Secretary, and Treasurer, who,
together with three other persons, shall constitute a board
of trustees.

ARTICLE III.

The object of the association shall be to encourage
the freedmen of the Southern States to emigrate to the
Northern and Western States and Territories, and settle
upon government lands, where they can be protected,
and live under laws in harmony with the Constitution of
the United States; or form townships of their own on
the New England plan, with churches, schools, &c.,
according to their own predilections.

ARTICLE IV.

Every individual owning a farm not less than a quarter section, or forty acres, shall be entitled to membership in this association, by the payment of five dollars towards the general expenses. Any surplus remaining over and above the expenses will be invested in farms for poor families, who have always been loyal to the United States government.

ARTICLE V.

Every freedman who purchases a farm and settles upon the same, shall be an honorary member of this association, until he shall have paid for the same and obtained his deed, when he shall be admitted to full membership.

ARTICLE VI.

The officers of the Principia Club shall act as officers of this association, until an act of incorporation shall be obtained, or until other officers shall be elected.

APPENDIX.

If any proof were needed of the truth of our positions in the editorial, the preamble, the resolutions, or the necessity of the transfer of the freedmen from Southern rule and the barbarism of slavery, to the more civilized portions of the land, it may be found in the Appendix. The testimony of the Southern press is absolutely overwhelming. We might print a large volume of the same kind, but we content ourself with only specimens enough to answer our purpose, from both the Northern and Southern press, leaving the mass of testimony still in our drawer.

We begin this catalogue of witnesses with an article from the Boston "Traveller," which quotes and comments upon Southern testimony with so much truthfulness, that we give the article entire.

NEGROES AND THEIR RIGHTS.

The recent Democratic Convention of Edgefield County, South Carolina,— the home of "Hamburg" Butler,— adopted the following resolution :—

" We regard the issues between the white and the colored people of this State, and of the entire South, as an antagonism of race. not a difference of political parties. This State and the United States were settled by the white race ; the lands now belong to the white race ; the white race are responsible for its government and civilization, and white supremacy is essential to our continued existence as a people. We are willing to accord to the colored race equal and exact justice, and we recognize all of their rights and privileges under the laws of this land."

Rightly interpreted this means— "We will give the niggers all their rights, but really they have no rights." That is the old doctrine of the Democratic party, which changes its principles only when the leopard changes its spots, and a more truthful declaration of its principles than is often presented. Some of the Southern Democrats, who just now are endeavoring to secure negro votes for their party, deprecate these declarations. and the resolution has given rise to some discussion in the South Carolina press.

The Spartansburg " Spartan " says :—

" Unfortunately there are too many who, thinking they can manipulate the negro vote, wish to bring it into the Democratic party. If this is done it will not only destroy the controlling influences of the white man and endanger his institutions and civilization, but will put the up country of South Carolina under the control of the low country, where the great negro vote lies."

The Charleston " News," taking a different view of the case. says :—

" If colored people are willing to become Democrats in good faith, it will require grave deliberation to determine whether it is not wiser to let them in, and give them a voice in the party, than to leave them outside as a bait for Independent Democrats. The Independent, not the colored Democrat, is the rock ahead in South Carolina politics."

The "News" is willing to allow negroes to act in the Democratic party, it seems, solely because the colored vote may thereby be controlled. It does not concede their right to vote, and to vote as they may choose, but it realizes that some of them will vote, notwithstanding the opposition of the Spartan school of Democracy, and seeking to have that vote controlled in the interests of the party, it is willing to have it understood by the negroes that they will find no obstacles in the way of their voting, if they unite with the Democratic party. The same end is sought by the "Spartan" and by the "News." The first-named wishes to secure the supremacy of a race by preventing the negroes from voting, while the "News" thinks it a better policy to adopt measures for the control of their votes. The "News" is no more friendly to the colored men than its contemporary, and the policy it proposes is as dangerous to their rights, as that of those who, in an outspoken manner, tell the negroes they are entitled to no political privileges.

PLAIN TALK.—The Providence "Journal" says : "The stipulations to which the Southern States solemnly pledged themselves, as the conditions of restoration to their forfeited rights in the Union, and to their readmission to a share in the government which they had attempted to overthrow, have been shamelessly violated. The negro is not permitted to vote unless he is frightened into voting the Democratic ticket. He has practically 'no rights which a white man is bound to respect.' In some of these States a sort of peonage has been established, which differs from slavery mainly in the exemption of the master from the care of the slave in sickness and old age, and in all of them disqualifying laws, and still more disqualifying practices under the laws, prevail. History presents no parallel to the forbearance shown by the conquering party in the rebellion, and none to the perfidy of the party that was overcome."

A leading paper in the State of Senator Gordon — the Columbus " Enquirer-Sun," — thus favors the lynch law : " A good, able-bodied, healthy corpse, or even a slightly damaged one, dangling from the limb of a tree on a public highway, strikes more terror into the heart of a criminal, and creates more respect for the fiat of justice, than the inside of a thousand jails, or the presence of an army of judges and jurymen. There is an appalling grandeur, a horrifying sublimity in the spectacle of a ghastly, half-devoured human form suspended in mid-air, receiving alike unconsciously the refreshing drops of the nocturnal dew that gives life to the violets, or the glowing rays of the morning sun as it ascends the eastern horizon and beams smilingly down on a busy world."

Which is correct? Here is Representative Waddell of North Carolina, formerly a rebel general, telling an organization of Union veterans, that not one person in one hundred thousand in the South expects or desires compensation for property destroyed by the Union armies, and here is ex-editor Cheney of Lebanon, who has travelled through the South and sojourned in Florida, saying : " You meet with no man in the South who does not either earnestly assert the justice of these claims, or leave with you the impression that he hopes they will be paid, because such payment means more money and greater prosperity for the South. Even the negroes, when it comes to the test, will be found co-operating with their masters to secure compensation for their own freedom." We repeat our question, Which is correct? — *Concord Monitor.*

LOUISIANA.

Ex-Governor Pinchbeck had an interview with the President recently, in which he took occasion to express his views concerning the needs of Louisiana. He represents the interview to have been pleasant and satisfactory. Pinchbeck says the State has now the best governor of any other within his recollection ; that the people were generally better satisfied than heretofore, with the condition of affairs, although the people there, as elsewhere,

complain of hard times. The only thing of which Pinchbeck complains is that the few children, nearly white,
in the public schools in New Orleans, have been required
to leave them. They should, he said, have been permitted
to remain until faded out by increase of years. His own
children were included in the number removed by the
school authorities.

THE SOUTHERN POLICY.

The Principia Club of Cambridgeport has just published
a pamphlet of 160 pages with the above title, containing
a history of the President's Southern policy, so far as
developed, up to the close of the extra session of Congress. The facts and testimony were collated by its
president, and constitute a chain of evidence absolutely
overwhelming to all but the conspirators, who are determined to ignore the facts and swear it through in the
interest of the bull-dozed Democracy. That the said
policy is a failure to promote Republicanism, can no
longer be doubted. That it has put the government of
the country into the power of the conspirators is abun-
dantly proved by this pamphlet, which will be read with
great interest.— *Traveller.*

The colored people of the South are physically and
socially in a worse condition to-day than when held in
the bonds of slavery, and as citizens their badge of
citizenship is a mockery, and far more galling than the
chains which bound them in involuntary servitude. The
Constitution promises them protection in equal rights
before the law as citizens, but the protecting arm of the
Federal power has been withdrawn, and the written law
is not worth the parchment on which it is inscribed.
The guarantees of the Constitution are suspended. The
rights of citizenship are a baseless dream. The heel of
political oppression is planted upon their citizenship with
a power as ruthless as that which restrained their physi-
cal freedom as men. The Constitution and its guarantees have become a mere sham.— *Washington Republican.*

The grand jury of Pike County, Miss., reported that
many persons summoned before them as witnesses failed

to come, because of the fear of personal violence should
they testify. "One witness," they say, "was assassi-
nated while *en route* to the seat of justice, and we have
received such information as to lead us to believe that
the lives of others would be in danger, if they came
before the court to testify." Mississippi gives a Democratic majority of fifty thousand. — *Chicago Inter-Ocean.*

But what right has the "Inter-Ocean" to complain?
Hasn't the policy given Mississippi peace? Haven't the
bull-dozers been informed that they will be conciliated,
regardless of expense? And what is the importance of
a murder or two, or the perversion of justice, or any
other little violation of the Declaration of Independence
and the Constitution, compared with peace and reform?
The "Inter-Ocean" is an implacable newspaper, and
ought to be ashamed of itself for printing such bloody-
shirt facts, and insinuating unkind things against the
President and his Democratic policy ! — *Traveller.*

Alluding to the suggestion of a Southern paper that
Mr. Garrison should be hung, the Philadelphia "Bulletin" says : "It is difficult to say with certainty what may
not happen in a country the government of which is now
controlled by a political party which once strove to
destroy it ; but we have a very strong notion that when
hanging for treason begins in this country Mr. Garrison
will not be the first victim. If such a policy should be
suddenly introduced, it would vacate about three-fourths
of the Democratic seats in Congress and rob the Democratic party of its most popular leaders."

We know what we are talking about, and we say this
is the plan which Western and Southern Democrats are
now working up. Their first purpose is to capture the
government, and their next will be the separation of the
States. Mr. Voorhees's statesmanship does not recognize any community of interest between the West and
the East. He thinks "the great West" and "the sunny
South" should join hands and let the Eastern States
with their "capitalists" and "bondholders" and "Shy-
locks" go. This is the new Democratic scheme, and it

is one that honest men and patriots must fight from the start. — *Indianapolis Journal.*

The Atlanta "Constitution" objects to the roasting of negroes alive in Alabama, especially those who have not been convicted of crime. Alluding to a recent affair in that State, it says : "No immigrant, looking for a new home. will for a moment think of settling in a State or section that permits mobs to supersede courts. The senseless burning of Owen Wright may cost the cotton State a million of dollars, coming as it did at a time when immigrants were looking this way from the Northern States."

The Meriden, Miss., "Mercury," supports the policy by declaring that "no man should be tolerated as an independent candidate for any cause and under any circumstances, who attempts to procure his election by solidly arraying the black voters in his favor," and the Okolona, Miss., "Southern States," supplements this with the following : "The real. simon-pure Democracy of Mississippi, have never made the negro any promises — none whatever. We have, therefore, no pledges to redeem. Remember that. We will see that he is protected in his life, limb, and property as far as in us lies ; but at the same time we will take precious pains to nip any of his political aspirations in the bud. 'This is a white man's government, made for white men and their posterity forever.'" We congratulate the administration on the progress of the policy.

There are strong Republican districts in South Carolina, Mississippi, and Louisiana. Let Matthews, Hoar, Foster, and the other distinguished gentlemen who championed "the policy" in the Senate and House, together with the editors who have been "writing it up," go down there and help the Republicans elect the right kind of men. There is no easier and better way to secure a Republican majority in the House. — *Inter-Ocean.*

At the Virginia election last week, the Republicans cast seven votes in Petersburg and three in Richmond. The "Washington Republican" says : "It is well known that the negro loves the franchise and is proud to exercise it. The only reason for his not having done so at the recent election was that he could not safely vote as he wished, and would not vote the other ticket."

Alluding to the Atlanta speech of President Hayes, William Lloyd Garrison says : " The mental obfuscation of the President is hard to parallel ; but his moral standard in this instance, is as flexible as ' a reed shaken by the wind.' Such a confounding of loyalty and treason, right and wrong, liberty and slavery, and treating them all ' with respect,' and in the same complimentary manner, is enough ' to stir a fever in the blood of age.' Hail, Judas Iscariot! Hail, Benedict Arnold! Your reproach shall now be taken away! You nobly acted up to your ' convictions,' and are as much entitled to commendation as the apostle John or the patriot George Washington! We humbly beseech you to be ' equally liberal and generous and just' to the apostle and patriot aforesaid, who were not less heroic and true to their convictions. Neither party has anything to be ashamed of; but both glory in their achievements.".

The sum total of Democratic policy in the South is the condign punishment of venial crime committed by Republicans and negroes, and amnesty for all crimes committed by Democrats. The Democratic party has never been strong enough anywhere to declare its independence of the dangerous classes. — *Philadelphia North American.*

The Atlanta "Independent," in discussing the question of who saved Georgia to the Democrats, does not give credit to Benjamin Hill, but to the shot-guns of the Ku-Klux. — *Cincinnati Gazette.*

GOING TO LEAVE " OLD MISSISSIPPI."

Senator Bruce, colored, of Mississippi, is preparing to shake the dust of that unfriendly stronghold of Democracy from his feet. He realizes that it is not the place where a black man can safely go to grow up with the country. His marriage to a Cleveland belle was only part of the programme he has mapped out for himself.

He has bought considerable property in that vicinity,
and when his senatorial term has expired he will go to
his farms, and let others fight it out on the color line.

HAMPTON'S LEGION OF "CONCILIATORS."

The "Traveller" has all along maintained, in spite of
the protests of the Northern doughfaces who worship
the ex-Confederate chiefs, that the conciliatory profession of Hampton & Co. is a malicious snare, and the
fraternal disposition attributed to their followers is a
delusion. As the campaign at the South advances, the
truth begins to develop, and even the Northern conciliators begin to acknowledge it. The following information comes in the form of a Washington despatch to one
of the most obedient newspaper servants of the Southern
chieftains : —

Terrorism in South Carolina.

Information from Abbeville District, in South Carolina, is to the effect that Democrats have already begun
a system of terrorism to prevent Republicans from organizing for political purposes. Several of the local
papers of that section are charging that Republicans of
that vicinity have completed a ticket, and that it is already being circulated secretly among colored voters,
and upon this curious charge an attempt is being made
to stir up white citizens to take this matter in hand, and
act in time, and vigorously. In Edgefield District, one
of the local newspapers, in commenting upon this reported secret action on the part of the Republicans, says
that something is feared in Edgefield County, and upon
this urges that two Republicans, who are supposed to be
leaders in this movement, should, if they dared to lift
their heads or fingers in political machinations, be seized
and hung. To use its own words : "Yes, we mean exactly what we say. If those named, and others, ever dare
to inaugurate political schemes in Edgefield again, let us
hang them. Not only our own self-respect, but our
safety demands it, and that without masks or disguise."

. The newspaper quoted is the Edgefield "Advertiser,"
which contains a long article giving the names of those

3

Republicans against whom it tries to incite the mob. The Abbeville "Medium" joins in the cry against the Republicans, who are exercising their common rights, and advises the Democrats to "throw out pickets" in order to suppress the movement. What all this talk means everybody knows, and the experience of the Southern Republicans shows them what they are to expect if they dare to exercise their privileges as citizens. Extraordinary emphasis is given to this revival of Ku-Kluxism, by the recollection that it is just two years since the horrors of the Hamburg massacre were enacted, on the very ground where this movement finds its inspiration, under the patronage of one who now holds a seat in the United States Senate; and that it is more than one year since the State government of South Carolina was surrendered to Hampton with the assurance that everybody's rights would be protected, and that fraternal relations would be maintained as a result of the conciliatory policy. This melancholy failure of all efforts to compromise with the perfidious ex-Confederates, in South Carolina, is only one in a score of lessons, by which the North has blindly failed to profit. The assassins, who slaughtered the colored Republicans, at Hamburg, are still at large, and ready for more bloody work; and Hampton sits calmly at the head of affairs in his State, deluding the people of the North with promises which he never intends to fulfil. It would seem to be about time for us to recall the language of the Cincinnati platform, declaring it to be " the solemn obligation of the legislative and executive departments of the government " to " secure to every citizen complete liberty and exact equality in the exercise of all civil, political, and public rights." This language was enforced by the imperative demand for " a Congress and a chief executive whose courage and fidelity to these duties shall not falter until these results are placed beyond dispute or recall." It is useless to deny that the signs are ominous in the South. The time seems to have arrived for testing the courage and fidelity of those whom the Republican party called to the duty of protecting the rights of citizenship, and the capability of Republican institutions for the plainest purposes and requirements of a government.

The Portland "Advertiser," a disgruntled sheet of Republican antecedents, says President Hayes has effected a "permenant settlement of the Southern question." That depends. He has secured Democratic ascendency in every Southern State. He has wiped out the Republican party of the South. He has rewarded bull-dozers instead of punishing them for their crimes. He has emasculated the United States flag so that it is no longer the symbol of protection to the newly enfranchised race. But the one thing which would compensate in some degree for these acts, he has not been able to do ; viz., make loyal men of the unreconstructed ex-rebels. These are just as bitter, venomous, and implacable today as on the day when Gen. Grant's term of office expired. One man, and one only, so far as we know, has been changed by the "new departure," and that man is now a Cabinet officer. Upon the same terms even the Chisholm assassins might be conciliated.—*Concord Monitor.*

The safest thing to do with the Southern claims of all kinds is to reject them promptly. If the entire batch should be ruled out, some deserving persons might suffer, but the country would be saved the cost of enriching a good many scores of rascally rebels. The claims now on file foot up about three hundred millions of dollars, and we venture to say that not half a million of this amount is honestly due to the claimants.—*Philadelphia Bulletin.*

The lynching of the colored man, Walker Denning, in the town of Riverside, Texas, appears to have been an unusually brutal and unjustifiable act, even for Texas. The girl with whom he eloped admitted to the reporter of a Texas paper that she prompted his course, Denning at first strongly objecting and advising her to stay at home. The spectacle of twenty armed men firing buckshot into a chained and helpless victim at such close range that his clothing was set on fire, horrifies us with its unnecessary savagery, But the revelation is no new one. We have already had proof upon proof that under "conciliation" there is no law, justice, nor mercy for the unfortunate colored people of the South; and this merely adds another to the long list of butcheries, and worse than Turkish barbarities, of which the blood-thirsty rebel element have been guilty.—*Traveller.*

Henrietta Wood, a colored woman, of Cincinnati, has recovered two thousand five hundred dollars damages against ex-Sheriff Ward, of Campbell County, Kentucky, for unlawful duress and abduction. In 1853, when living in Cincinnati, she was enticed over the river to Kentucky, and delivered over to Ward, who kept her as a slave seven months, when he disposed of her to a slave-trader. She was sold South, and remained fifteen years in slavery. She returned to Cincinnati after the close of the war, and commenced the action which has just terminated in her favor.

The "Macon (Ga.) Telegraph" demands that the Southern people shall be paid for · their emancipated slaves. Next they will probably want pay, at hotel rates, for the entertainment of Union prisoners during the war. — *Philadelphia Press.*

The colored Republicans in Somerville County, South Carolina, carried the local election recently by a large majority, but the Democrats managed to count them out, on the ground that it wouldn't do for the Republicans to carry the first election of the season. — *Journal.*

And this right under the much-praised administrative system of Wade Hampton, who, with Gordon, Lamar, Stephens, Hill, and the rest of the treasonable species, constitutes the organic beau-ideal of statesmanship. Turn the other cheek and let them slap it, Mr. Journal.

A SAD, TRUE STORY. — A letter from New Orleans to the "Philadelphia Press" thus refers to the native Republicans of Louisiana : —

"The leaders were beset with dangers and difficulties such as have never even been dreamed of in the North. One by one they have given their life's blood in the cause.

They have lain down their lives, true to the flag. They have been thinned out by assassination and violence. Their graves — the graves of the victims of Democratic outrage — are scattered throughout the South. There are comparatively few of the living to tell the tale. A large proportion of these, even, have been maimed and crippled in the fight.

They are to-day, as a rule, none the less true to the Republican faith. The Southern Republican leaders have nothing to offer by way of palliation or excuse. They have fallen one by one in the enemy's front. The Republican masses have been massacred by wholesale; have been murdered and outraged upon every occasion and in every manner. They have been hunted as the beasts of the jungle. Their blood cries to Heaven from every hillside, from every by-way, and from every bridle-path in the South. There has been more of blood — *Republican blood* — that has dyed the soil of Louisiana alone than all that has been shed in all of the Indian wars of a quarter of a century. It has been shed, alas, in vain. *The American people were not a nation. There was not, there is not to-day, to their shame be it said, the power within the American people, to protect the life, or avenge the murder of an American citizen, within the American lines."*

We would crucify our extreme modesty and suggest to the above writer the reason why "there is not to-day the power within the American people to protect the life or avenge the murder of an American citizen." Is it not because we, "the people," put their political power into the hands of the commander-in-chief of our army, in trust for four years, who betrayed that trust by the transfer of that power into the hands of a contemptible knot of armed and defiant rebels, thus constituting a solid South with which to rule the nation? And is it not because the said commander-in-chief, at the demand of the said rebels in arms, packed up his traps and withdrew our "federal bayonets" from the South, thus giving them, in addition to *their* State rule, *our* national su-

premacy, by further giving them two States with large
Republican majorities?

And furthermore, is it not because the loyal North did
not arise as one man and demand the impeachment of
the traitor who bartered their liberties for a *sham* peace,
taking rebel promises for pay which have since been
repudiated?

But the men who assisted the President in this nefari-
ous business are coming to their senses. In a speech a
few days ago, at Toledo, O., the Hon. Charles Foster,
M. C. from Ohio, and a member of the political firm of
Matthews, Foster & Co., renounces the Southern policy
of the administration, which that firm helped to inaugurate, as follows : —

"I believed in and supported President Hayes in the
policy of refusing the use of force to sustain State gov-
ernments. I believed in it as a matter of principle,
though his course can be sustained on the ground of
necessity. I had hoped that his policy of kindness and
conciliation would result in the formation of a public
sentiment South that would permit Republicans to exercise fully all of the political rights guaranteed to them
by the Constitution and the amendments thereto. Know-
ing that there are a large number of the people South
who are tired of the Bourbon Democracy, I hoped that
the President's course would permit them the more easily
to assert themselves in some form in opposition to the
Democracy. I see signs of a realization of this hope,
especially in the States of Tennessee, North Carolina,
and Texas, but in less permanent form than I had hoped.
The President's policy has lost him the sympathy of the
great mass of his party. That he has conscientiously
done his duty as he saw it, there can be no question.
No matter whether the conventions indorse him or not,
no man will rejoice more than he over Republican success — North and South. While he was beslavered with
praise from the Southern Democracy, they seemed to be
laying broad and deep the foundations for a solid South.
Upon the attempt, through the Potter resolutions, to
unseat the President, they, with bare two exceptions,

voted for it. They declined even to give an opportunity to vote upon the Hale amendment, which would have permitted an investigation into Democratic frauds. Jeff Davis makes as treasonable speeches as those of 1861, and he receives the indorsement and approval of a large proportion of the press and people. Out of one hundred newspapers in Mississippi, ninety-five indorse and applaud Jeff Davis. Mr. Singleton, of the same State, on the floor of the House of Representatives, declared ' his highest allegiance to be due to his State, both in peace and in war.'

" By the adoption of the Fifteenth Amendment, the political power of the South in the Electoral College and the House of Representatives, was increased about forty per cent. The Republican party to-day can poll, if permitted to do so, forty per cent. of the vote of the South. Yet, in the coming elections, I do not believe that we can carry one in five of the districts that we know to be reliably Republican. By force and fraud the political power of forty per cent. of their people is exercised solely by the sixty per cent., thus making a solid Democratic South. The right of the citizens of the several States to enjoy the privileges and immunities of all the States is not respected in many localities. It is said, condescendingly, that a Republican can live in the South without trouble, if he will keep a padlock on his mouth.

" Now, my fellow-citizens, there can be no lasting peace until the amendments to the Constitution are executed in good faith, both in letter and spirit. A solid South is a constant menace to the peace of the country. It means that the Constitutional amendments shall be abrogated and repealed in spirit; it means the usurpation by the majority of all the political power of one section of the country, and with a fragment of the other section it enables the solid South, inspired as it is by the spirit and the men who sought the overthrow of the country, to now rule and control it; and yet they may be in a large minority in the whole country. Such success, if it is submitted to, means the payment of the rebel claims, the pensioning of rebel soldiers, the payment for slaves lost in rebellion. I feel it my especial duty to say that as long as the menace of the solid South threatens the peace of the country, it is the duty of the North to be united against it. I am desirous as any man can be that we shall get away from sectional politics, but I cannot close my eyes to the danger of a solid South. The advice I give is simply that ordinary prudence and care be exercised. I repeat, that so long as the menace of a solid South exists, it is the duty of the North to continue to meet it with ‘ the most Greeks.’ ”

The New Orleans “ Times ” says : “ While the North, with a lavish hand, is soothing the fevered brow of the Southern suffering, she is building a monument of gratitude which will be luminous forever.” And the only thing the North will ask in return for what it cheerfully gives is that the monument shall bear the inscription, “ Justice to all men.”

Senator Chaffee, of Colorado, who is now at Saratoga, was asked if he expected an early revival of business, and in response said : “ Yes ; a beginning of a revival, because the excessively hard times and real hunger have driven the lazy to work. I was at Hot Springs, Ark., not long ago, and saw thousands of people going through to Texas. As many as twelve hundred emigrants would go through Arkansas in a day. I talked to many of them, and they told me that they had not generally twenty-five dollars ahead of the railroad fare, but said that they desired to get a piece of ground, raise potatoes, or anything, and be independent. That is what will bring us up, and nothing else, every idle person to do something at production.

RECENT BULL-DOZING IN LOUISIANA.

The Pointe Coupee, La., “ Record,” a Democratic paper, on the 17th inst., said : —

“ It is rumored that several men from Bayou Fordoche came to the court house this morning to make affidavits against certain parties from that section of the parish. The complaint is shooting and whipping.”

Commenting on this, the New Orleans "Observer" of the 24th said :—

"From sources absolutely reliable, affecting affairs in Pointe Coupee parish, we learn that since the hanging of four black men in the Racourcee settlement by the bulldozers of that section, the colored people thereabouts have sought to leave the locality, going to Fordoche, a bayou neighborhood where is a large colored settlement of small farmers.

"Determined to stop this migration of colored people, and at the same time terrorize the Fordoche farmers, on the night of the 14th inst., Wednesday, a crowd of bulldozers, some sixty odd men from Racourcee, came to this colored settlement, and for no known cause, save that which we have expressed, outraged several inoffensive and hard-working colored people. Lucy Allain, a colored woman, was stripped and whipped unmercifully, and the same treatment was given William Abraham. Levi Sherman was shot three times. All three of these victims are now confined, by reason of this outrage, to their beds. Others of the colored people would have received like treatment, but they got out of the way. A prisoner in the jail there was hung for sport. Fortunately, he was cut down in time to save his life. Some colored people were outraged, and atrocities and indignities practised generally befitting the lawless character of the Democratic party-workers and bull-dozers. The good citizens (white) of the locality have called a mass meeting to express their indignation and to attempt to redress these wrongs, or at least put a stop to further outrages. The meeting was to have had place on Wednesday, the 21st inst. A similar meeting was also called for the same day at New Roads. The information furnished us of these horrible crimes is from purely Democratic sources, gentlemen and decent citizens who abhor the partisan atrocities of their party-workers. So far as we can learn, Republicans of Pointe Coupee are so terrorized that even prominent gentlemen there will say nothing of this act of atrocity, the information in fact reaching this city and our office from responsible Democratic citizens. We are informed that the plantation visited was one of the New York Warehouse and Security Company's places. and of which Mr. Bradish Johnson is the agent.

The Macon, Ga.. "Telegraph" is only a little in advance of the ex-Confederate "conservatives" when it demands the repeal of the fourteenth amendment, that the Southern people may extort payment for their liberated slaves. That will soon be one of the regular planks in the Southern Democratic platform.

In Jasper County, Georgia, since the war (reports a local paper), there have been sixty-nine men killed, and not a single hanging.

The Augusta (Ga.) "Chronicle" suggests that the proper place for Congressman Rainey (the man whose sobriety enabled Congress to adjourn on the day appointed) is the chain-gang. Perhaps his consignment to a slave-gang would suit the "Chronicle" better.

The Democrats claim that white and colored school children have equal school privileges in Georgia, but this is far from being true. In Atlanta. there are fine houses for the white scholars ; the colored scholars are sent to cellars and other unfit places, and are limited in accommodation at that.

The Charleston "News and Courier" is Wade Hampton's organ. and it is leading his campaign in South Carolina. Alarmed because the Republicans threatened to exercise their right to talk politics and vote, the organ says : " Seceders and malcontents will be treated as public enemies, and made political outcasts. The Democratic party will not lay down the sceptre of authority in South Carolina, nor shall the sceptre be wrested from the strong hands by which it is grasped." That is, Wade Hampton says, in substance, " I am for conciliating those who vote for me, but death to all who oppose!" Truly, as Gov. Boutwell said in his Maine speech, the Southern question is given the greater importance in this campaign by the action of the ex-rebels.

In North Carolina, the Republican leaders are trying to induce the negroes to vote by telling them that the coming election will be a fair and free one. The deception is not justifiable, and will cost the men who resort to it the confidence of the colored voters.

The vote for the Democratic State ticket last week was about eighty thousand. There was no opposition. The legislature will be almost entirely Democratic. — *Despatch from Alabama.*

And where, pray, is that new Independent party; where are the old Whigs, the administration Democrats, not to say anything about the resuscitated Republicans, who were to arise from the policy of conciliation? Alabama is pretty solid.

To deprive man of the fruit of his labors is to cut the sinews of industry. Who will care to labor if another is to appropriate the results of his toil? He is deprived of an inalienable right, the enjoyment of which alone can induce him to exercise the self-denial implied in labor and economy. To distribute the products of his industry to the community, as some social theorists would teach us, is to destroy individual enterprise, and to reduce society to a great almshouse. — *Zion's Herald.*

[Despatch to the Traveller.]

FREEDOM OF SPEECH NOT TOLERATED IN SOUTH CAROLINA.

"NEW YORK. Oct. 15. — A Washington despatch says that Congressmen Smalls and Rainey have been obliged to flee from South Carolina on account of their activity in organizing Republican meetings, and they were yesterday promised protection by the President."

Protection where? in Washington or South Carolina? It cannot be in the latter, for the President has put his "Federal bayonets" into the hands of Gov. (?) Hampton, and voluntarily shut himself out of that State. Nay, more, he has driven the bolts through his military power as commander-in-chief of the nation, and the last Congress screwed on the nut, which leaves the President powerless, and the Governor all-powerful. Let us see how he is using that power. The Democratic paper of

Sumter County, edited by one of the aids of Wade
Hampton, calls upon the Democrats to turn out and
break up the Republican meetings in such appeals as the
following : —

"Men with mothers and wives ; men with sisters dear ;
men who expect to raise families in Sumter County, —
let your sons and daughters turn out on Saturday and
meet the thieves whom Sam Lee is gathering together
and attempting to fasten on us as our rulers and masters
in this county. Let everything be conducted on Saturday with military order, promptness, and decision. In
1861 our Southern braves left their homes and firesides
and encountered every conceivable bodily privation,
every danger, for a cause that dwarfs into perfect insig-
nificance in comparison with the Democratic cause in
this county to-day, and yet are there men who are so
ease-loving and unpatriotic that they will not turn out
on Saturday to meet the Republican thieves? If such
there be, go mark them well.

"Let Northern speakers come ; we intend to carry
Sumter County Democratic, at the next election, in
spite of the world, flesh, and the devil.

"Democrats should rally as one, on Saturday. He
who dallies is dastard. He who doubts is damned.

"Surely, no one, who is worthy of the name of man,
can hesitate, under such conditions, to take a hand on
Saturday."

The following, to the rifle clubs, is given as the programme for the Democrats, on Saturday, Oct. 19, the
day the Republican meetings are called for nomina-
tions : —

"Presidents of clubs are requested to report to county
chairman, who can be found at the rooms of the executive committee, in the rear of the town hall, up stairs.
The clubs will be earnestly enjoined, by those in authority, to remain in line and under command of their re-
spective presidents until they are turned over to some
higher officer, from whom they will receive orders during
the day."

Ex-Senator Swails, of Williamsburg County, and also deputy United States marshal, has committed the unpardonable sin against the Wade-Hampton, Hamburg-Butler, shot-gun Democracy, by speaking at Republican meetings, for which offence he has been twice shot at, and finally driven from the county, having been visited by the Democratic Executive Committee, accompanied by a band of Red Shirts or Rifle Clubs, and presented with these good Democratic resolutions : —

Resolved, That S. A. Swails be required to leave Williamsburg in ten days.

Resolved, That he is a high-handed robber.

Resolved, That he and his rioters be held responsible for all incendiarism which may happen.

Resolved, That unless the above be complied with, he must forfeit his life.

These facts were yesterday brought to the attention of the President by Congressman Rainey and Mr. Swails, and it is reported that he thinks something ought to be done about it, and says just what the man whom he made Governor of South Carolina said : " Tell the people they shall have all the protection the law can give." Wade Hampton has the power to fulfil his promise, and it is apparent he never intended to give the Republicans the protection they asked, and we fear that President Hayes is putting them off with a promise of the protection he is well aware he cannot give.

These South Carolinians come to Washington and claim government protection to their persons and property while in the exercise of their constitutional political rights. The President " thinks something ought to be done about it " ! Wonderful ! So does an old hen when the hawks are after her chickens. But the difference between the two is this : the hen blusters about and immediately calls her subjects under her wings, thus giving them all the protection in her power. But the President *thinks something ought to be done*, but does nothing worthy of the occasion.

Wade Hampton promises " all the protection the law can give," and that was none at all while in his hands to

administer, for the reason that the theory of the shot-gun
Democracy is, that the negro has no *rights* that the
white man is bound to protect.

While the South is entitled to the palm of victory for
shot-gun Democracy, the North is a fair competitor for
doughface flunkeyism. Ex-Senator Swails, by the testimony of his personal friends in Boston, bears a character
the direct opposite of that given him in the following
paragraph from the Philadelphia "Times." While despotism is the rule in the South, owing to the natural soil
in which it is nurtured, we are happy to believe that
flunkyism *in the superlative degree* at the North is the
exception.

"If State Senator Swails of South Carolina, had lived
in any Northern State and prostituted his senatorial
office as openly and recklessly as is clearly proven he did
in that State, he would be in the penitentiary ; but having
resigned his seat to escape dismissal and fled to escape
punishment, he has settled down in Washington, where
a few carpet-bag thieves yet linger, and is telegraphing
over the country how the Hampton rifle clubs have driven
him from the State. As the South Carolina penitentiary
evidently haunts his dreams, he should hie himself to the
Massachusetts Botany Bay of public thieves, and put
himself under the protecting wing of Governor Rice.
He will find Kimpton there, and a fellow feeling will
make Kimpton wondrous kind to Swails."—*Philadelphia
Times.*

[Special Despatch to the Boston Traveller.]

WASHINGTON, D. C., Oct. 21.—The statement made to
the President, last week, by State Senator Swails, that
he was forced to leave South Carolina in consequence of
receiving a notice that his life would pay the penalty if
he remained, is fully confirmed by the Charleston "News
and Courier" received here to-day.

That paper admits that such a notice was served on
Swails, and says it was done because he was a dangerous
man, and disturbing the peace of the country where he
resided. Instead of lynching him the Democrats gave
him the opportunity of leaving the State.

The "News and Courier" contains an account of the capture of a Republican meeting at Lawtonville on Friday last, showing that the Democrats are determined to carry out their policy regardless of the instructions sent out by Attorney-General Devens to the U. S. officials.

The meeting was called by the Republicans in the interest of Smalls, the Republican candidate for re-election to Congress. The despatch to the " News and Courier," from Lawtonville, says :

" This morning the negroes began pouring in, attired in the recently-adopted radical uniform of blue shirts, several mounted clubs and other clubs on foot, embracing large numbers, being included. Fully 2,000 men, women and children gathered, when some eight red shirts galloped in and captured the meeting and proceeded to run it on a division of time schedule. Rousing Democratic speeches were made. Mr. Smalls failed to appear. Some of Hampton's men rode forty miles to hear Smalls. The effect of the day's work was exceedingly good."

Scott.

As goes South Carolina so go the other rebel States, as in the *first* rebellion. Georgia next falls into line after this fashion :

The " Augusta (Georgia) Constitutionalist" insists that the Democrats of South Carolina shall defy the lawful direction of the Attorney-General of the United States in regard to conspiracies against the political rights of the citizens, and shall continue to disturb, and, if need be, break up Republican meetings. The advice is equally plain and peremptory. Republicans are not to be allowed to hold meetings without the presence and participation of Democrats. What that participation is, is well understood. It is the attendance of armed men who will not allow a word said which does not meet with their approbation ; it is the warning of citizens not to join in the meetings ; it is the threatening of life if they do ; it is the savage assaulting of those who are conspicuous in proclaiming their intention to vote the Republican ticket ; it is armed and violent defiance of the law, and, in the last resort, assassination. The issue is clearly defined. It is, pure and simple, whether the government of the United States can and will protect its citizens in their constitutional rights, when those are rights which it is authorized and required to conserve and defend. Evidently the rebellion was not ended at Appomattox.— *Providence Journal.*

We have contemplated deferring the publication of this pamphlet until we could ascertain from the Secretary of the Interior the number of acres of unpre-empted land in each State, together with their location &c., &c., but we are informed by the commissioner of the land office in Washington that there are no data or statistics in his office that will give us that information.

As we may have to wait for Congress to assemble before we can obtain the necessary statistics, we shall send out our pamphlet at once, and set the ball in motion.

The question that has recently come up between the Secretary of the Interior and the Pacific railroads must be settled, so far as we can see, in favor of the Secretary, who has just issued a pamphlet with the grounds of his decision, and which has been sent us.

The railroads, however, may delay matters by their dilatoriness in making their returns to government of the lands sold by them, their location, &c., and it may be necessary for Congress to hurry up that matter a little, so that the land commissioner can give the desired information.

But there is no time to be lost. The " conciliated " Wade Hampton, and the Hamburg-massacre-Butler crowd have already organized the second rebellion in South Carolina, and armed their militia with "federal bayonets," over which waves the " bloody shirt," inscribed with Hampton's declaration in a speech in Sumter County, " that the Democrats must carry that county at all haz-ards," supplemented by Senator!! Butler, who " said it was unnecessary to tell them *how* to do it." " Webb," a correspondent of the Boston " Journal," tells us in the following paragraph, how they are doing it : —

SHAMEFUL CONDUCT OF THE MILITARY.

" Armed men have been stationed as pickets on roads leading to county conventions. These men were supplied with State arms, furnished through the United States, were evidently under good military discipline, had recognized officers, and were known as members of the State volunteer militia. At first they appeared without uniforms; of late they have attempted in uniform to break up Republican meetings. They have not hesitated to announce publicly that the white people of South Carolina had decided that Republican meetings should not be held, and that any attempt to hold such meetings might result in personal injury. At one of the meetings at Sumter County, one of the aids of Governor Hampton knocked the Republican chairman from the stand. Another seized the chairman by the throat and severely injured him. The speaker was Probate Judge Lee, who acted as chairman of the meeting, and who at that time was threatened both with shooting and hanging. So many authorized details of those acts of violence have been brought to the knowledge of the Administration here that the President and his Cabinet are convinced that there is an organized movement in South Carolina to put down by violence any attempt at Republican organization, and that Wade Hampton is giving this revolutionary and cowardly movement his active personal support. It is, perhaps, needless to say that the President is very much surprised at Hampton's conduct."

If " the President and his Cabinet " had consulted the Principia Club papers more, and Southern rebels less, it would not have taken them half of their Presidential term to learn that rebel promises are of no account whatever, for they would have discovered abundant evidence of their utter worthlessness. As " federal bayonets " are now so popular in *rebel* hands, and getting to be so useful to put down *Republicanism* in South Carolina, perhaps our verdant President, in his " *surprise*," may break the shackles with which he was voluntarily bound, and use " federal bayonets " to put down *rebellion*. At all events, he ought to obey the United States Constitution he has sworn to support, which tells him he "shall guarantee to every State in the Union a republican form of government." If he hasn't given away all his "federal bayonets" to the rebels, is it not about time for our commander-in-chief to use them in South Carolina? (See Principia Club Papers No. 7, pp. 152–5 : The Southern Policy.)

[Special Despatch to the Boston Traveller.]

WASHINGTON, D. C., Oct. 18. — The President has taken steps, through the proper officers, to have the outrage perpetrated at Sumter, South Carolina, investigated, with a view of ascertaining who is responsible, and whether or not there has not been an open violation of the United States laws.

District-Attorney Northrup has the case in charge, and will, said a member of the Cabinet to your correspondent to-day, make an energetic investigation of the outrage and report the facts promptly. There is no reason to doubt that he will do his whole duty and make a fearless investigation of the affair, which, according to the Democratic account, was brutal in the extreme. The Administration, said the Cabinet Minister further, will see that the rights of the colored people in South Carolina are maintained, and to this end will, if necessary, go to the full extent of the United States laws.

We may be too faithless in this matter, we hope we are, but when "investigations" shall result in the *punishment of criminals*, instead of their protection from further molestation, we may have more confidence that justice will triumph in rebeldom.

VIRGINIA COMES NEXT.

"President Hayes, who is attending an agricultural fair at Winchester, Virginia, made a hard money speech yesterday, and quoted Washington, Jefferson, Madison, and other distinguished Virginians in favor of sound money."—*Traveller, Oct. 17.*

While the President was making stump speeches in Winchester, in the direct line of civil service reform, as he understands it we suppose, the shot-gun brigade were at Hicksford demonstrating the fruits of his Southern policy. The "Traveller" states this case in the following strain of sarcasm.

A "saucy" negro was shot at Hicksford, Virginia, yesterday. It was a political meeting, of course. A Republican was speaking, and the negro had the audacity to applaud his sentiments. This was in the Court House. A leader of the Democracy named Reese, not wishing to soil the temple of justice with blood, called the negro out of the building and promptly shot him dead. There were four hundred colored men present and this shooting will be a lesson for them. They will now know better than to applaud Republican speakers, or vote a Republican ticket.

CONCLUSION.

We have thus spread out the present condition of the freedmen, before the American people. It is a plain case for the former, and not a hard one for the latter.

The whole question of emigration, as it now stands, lies in three propositions, one of which every freedman *must* choose.

1. He must remain, as he is, under the political trinity of despotism ; be denied the free ballot, conferred upon him by the amendments to the United States Constitution ; be forced to vote for the despotism that crushes him, already deserted by the government he fought to save, and which is constitutionally bound to protect him in his political rights and Christian privileges ; or,

2. He must, *vi et armis*, maintain those rights against rebel despotism, with the "Federal bayonets" in rebel hands, and the power to send the army to the Indians or the devil ; or,

3. He must, *quietly*, if he can, *forcibly*, if he must, emigrate to the public lands in the West, pre-empt a farm, and enjoy the rights of citizenship under a republican form of government, of which he is an integral part, and be represented in Congress by one elected by a majority of legal voters, and not by a minority of rebels,

as is now the case in large Republican districts in the Southern States.

For obvious reasons, we pray the freedmen, in Christ's stead, to be reconciled to the last proposition, and in every county and town where their political rights are ignored by a rebel Democracy, let them form colonies under a chosen leader and emigrate West. If they cannot go without assistance, let that fact be communicated to us, and we will appeal to the people of the North to furnish them the means to do so.

It will be readily perceived that the converse of all this will be, that the landed aristocracy of the South must pay their laborers honest wages, recognize their constitutional rights as citizens of this Republic, acknowledge the ownership of their capital, which means the fruits of their labor (land and labor being co-operative capital, neither being available or profitable without the other), or, otherwise, the land-owners must submit to the loss of their laborers by emigration, perform their own labor, or employ foreign emigrants.

NOTICE.

Five dollars will pay for *one hundred* of these pamphlets with the appendix, to be sent to as many freedmen in the Southern States, and constitute the donor a member of the Principia Club.

One dollar will pay for twenty copies of the same, sent as above.

Address the President of the Principia Club, J. W. ALDEN, No. 9 Hanson St., Boston, Mass.

☞ Read and Circulate.

ALBERT J. WRIGHT, Printer, 79 Milk Street (corner Federal), Boston.